D0998059

THIS WALKER BOOK BELONGS TO:

JN 03374178

First published 1985 by Walker Books Ltd
as *John Burningham's Colours*, *John Burningham's Opposites*,
John Burningham's a b c and *John Burningham's 123*
This edition published 1995

2 4 6 8 10 9 7 5 3

This book has been typeset in Goudy.
Printed in Hong Kong/China

British Library Cataloguing in Publication Data
A catalogue record for this book
is available from the British Library.
ISBN 0-7445-4320-7

JOHN BURNINGHAM

First Steps

Letters Numbers Colours Opposites

WALKER BOOKS
AND SUBSIDIARIES
LONDON • BOSTON • SYDNEY

Letters

a
alligator

b
bear

c
cow

d
duck

e
elephant

f
flowers

g goat

h hippopotamus

i ice cream

j juggler

k
kangaroo
l
lion

m monkey

n newt

o ostrich

p parrot

q queen

r rabbit

s snake

t

turtle

u

umbrella

V

violin

W

wasp

X xylophone
Y yak
Z zebra

Numbers

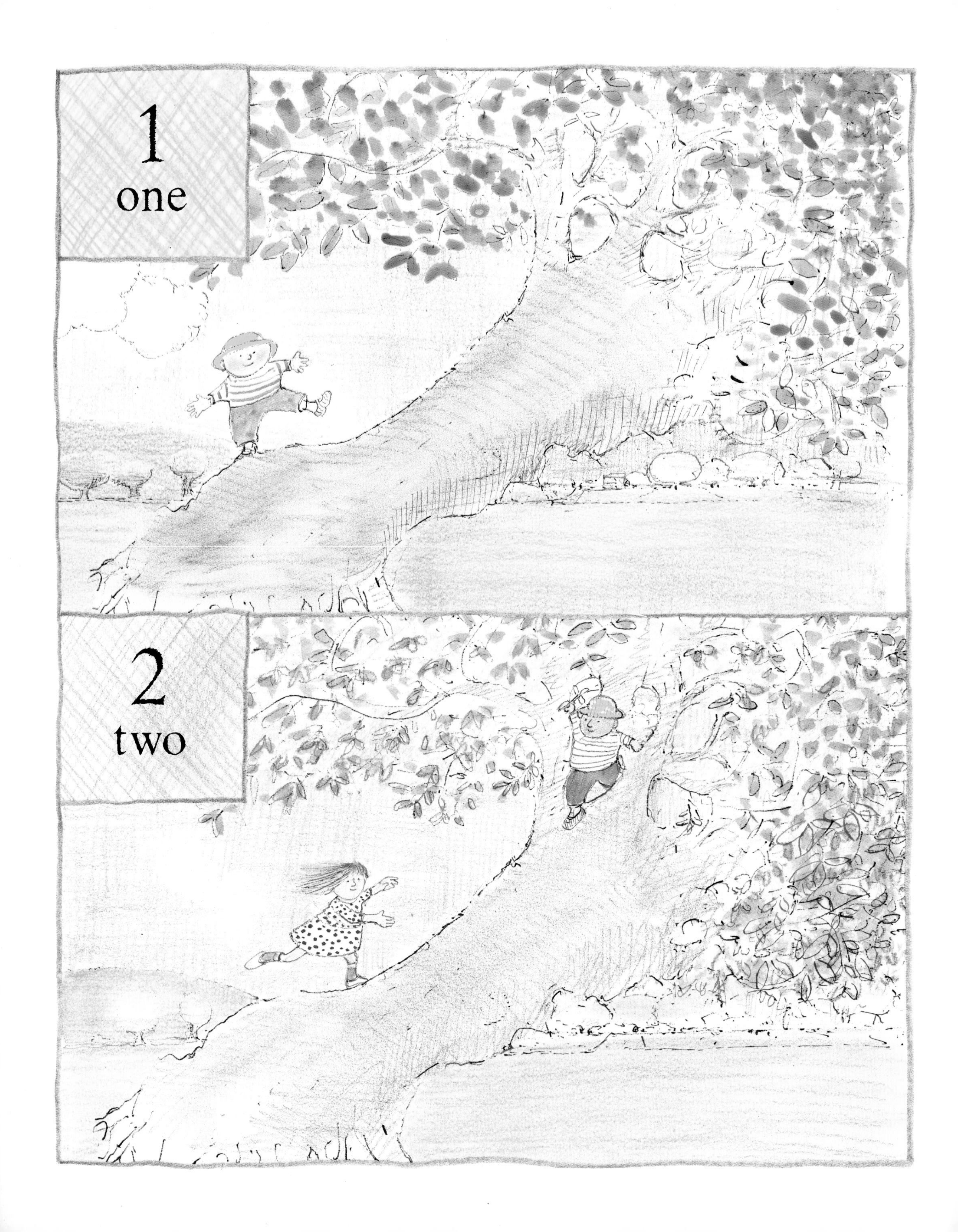
1
one
2
two

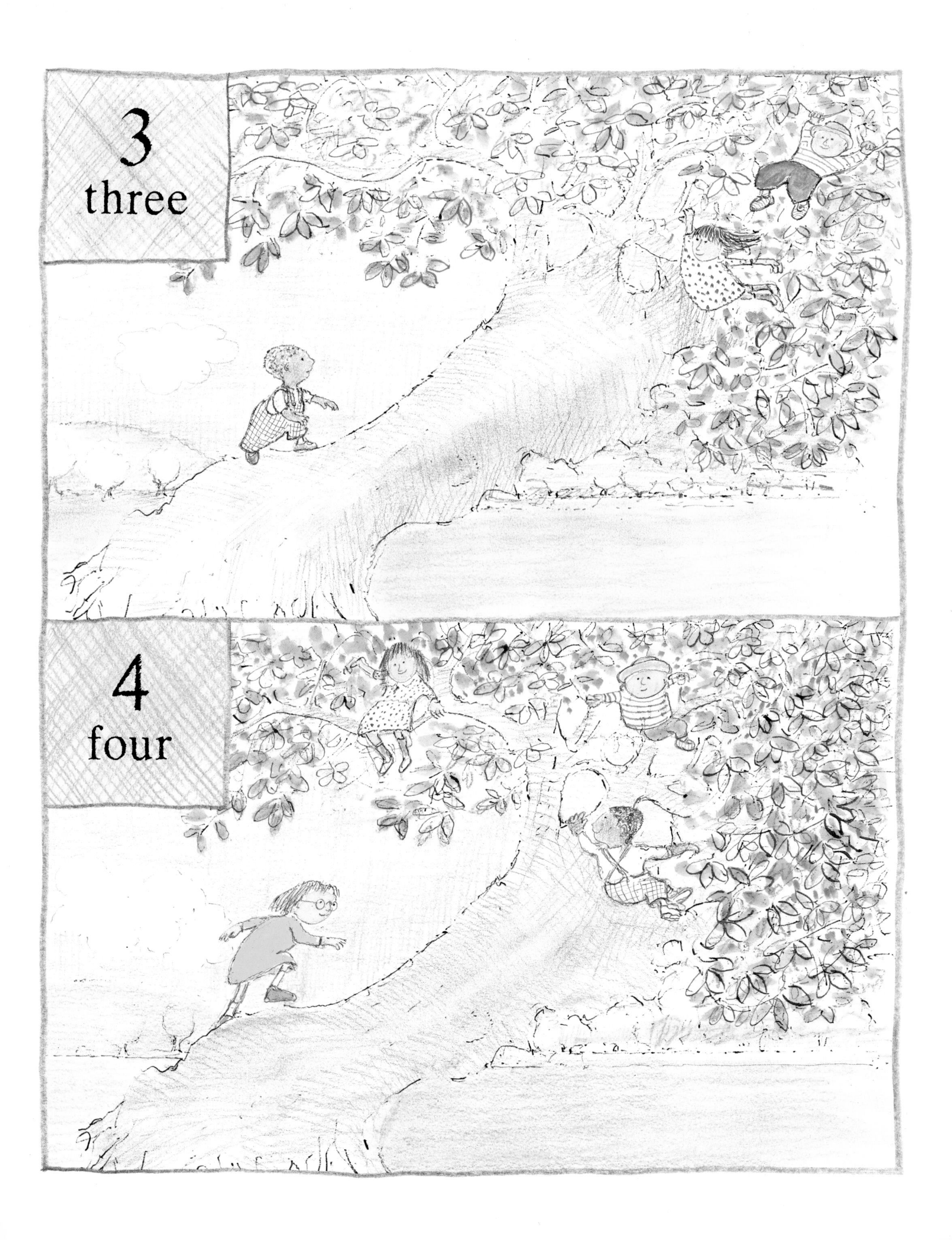
3
three
4
four

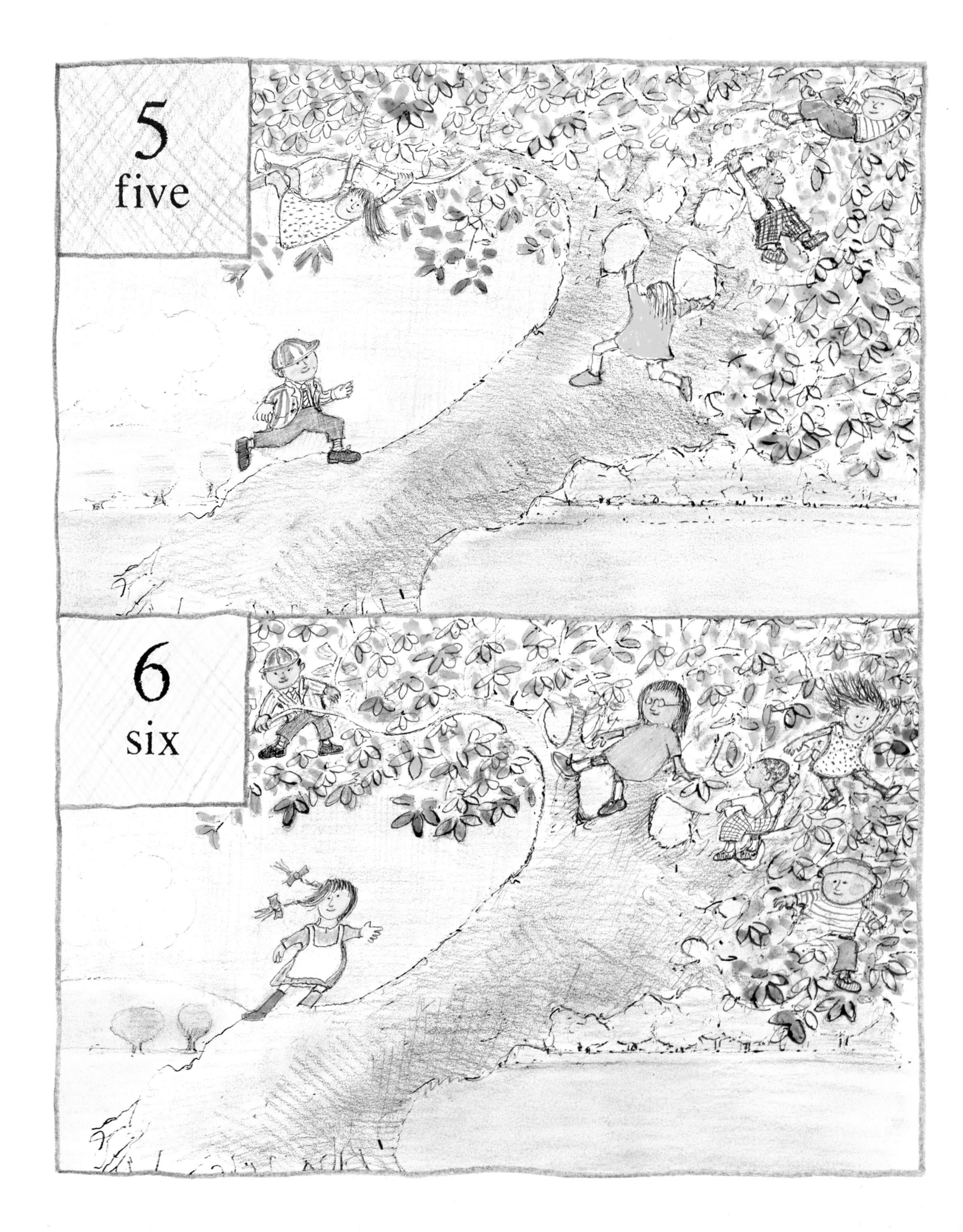
5
five
6
six

7
seven
8
eight

9
nine
10
ten

Colours

red

yellow

blue

purple

orange

green

white

black

red
yellow
blue
purple
orange
green
white
black

Opposites

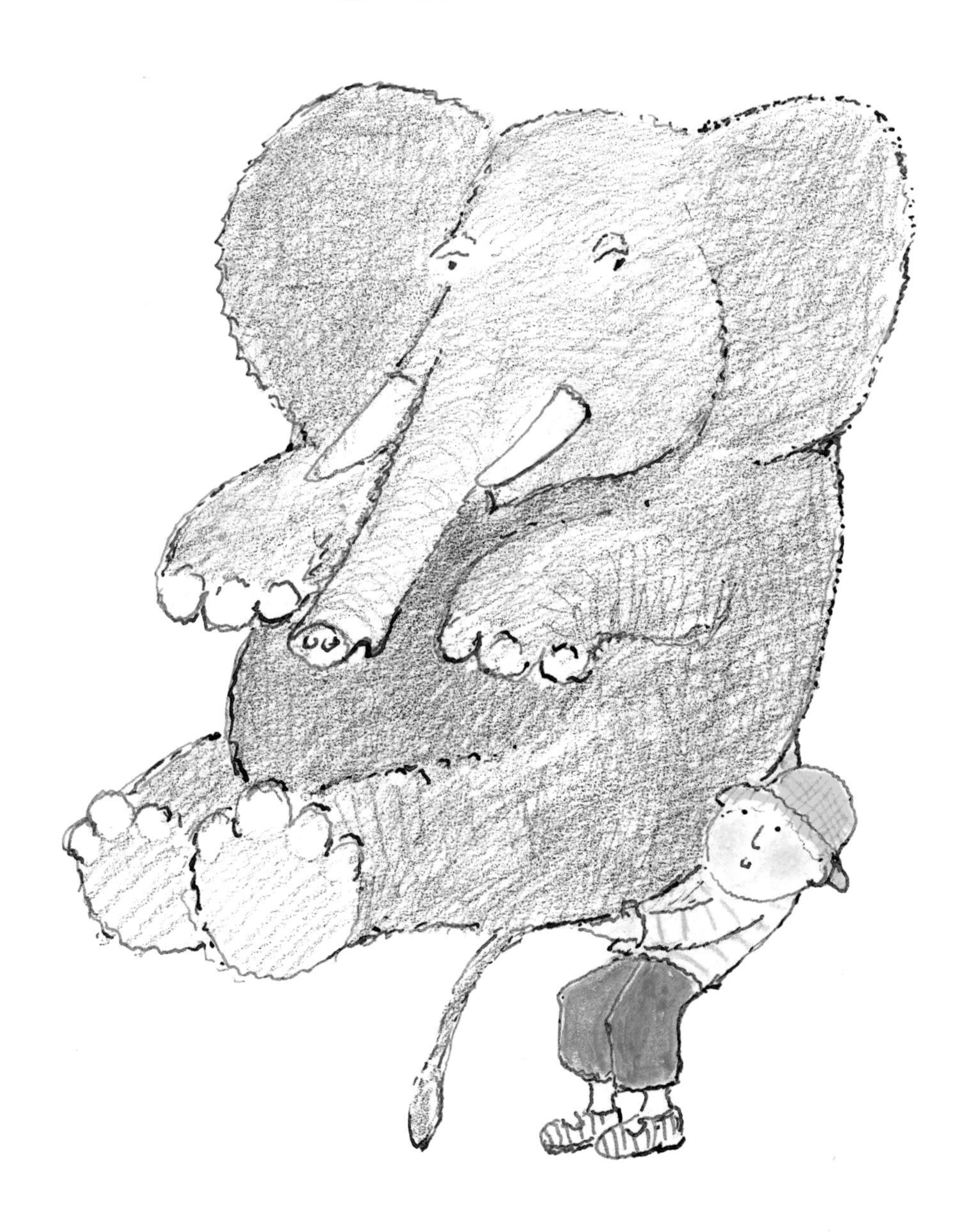

dry

wet

hard

soft

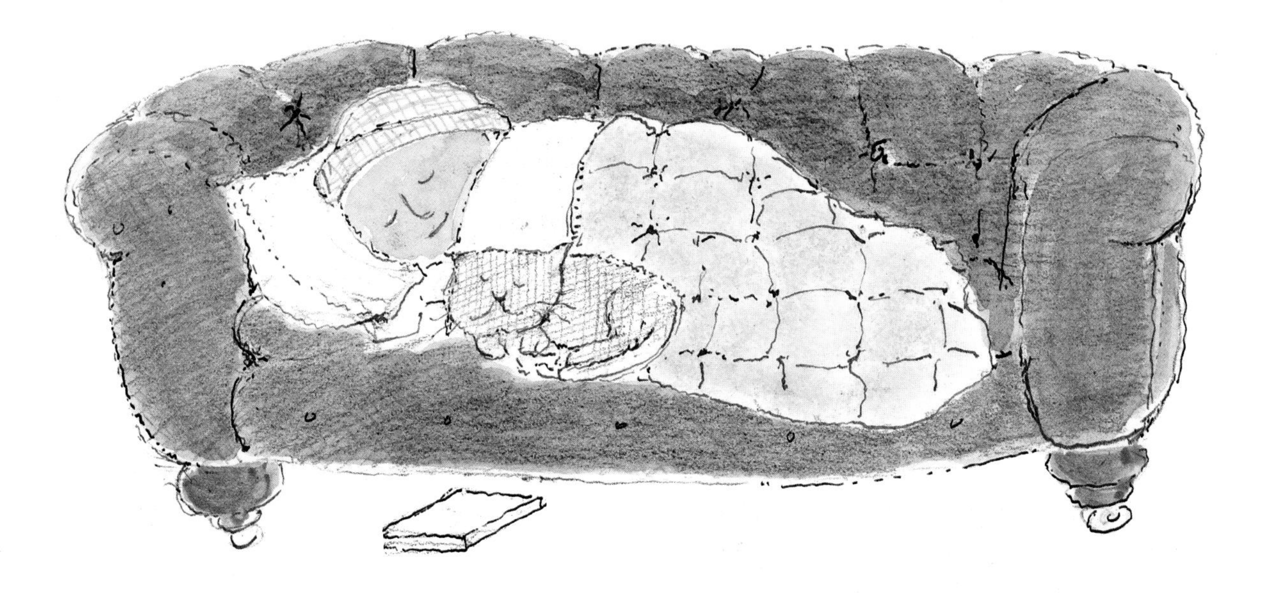

light

heavy

noisy

quiet

hot

cold

slow

fast

young

old

big

little

thin

fat

push
pull

open

shut